Constantinople Quilts

8 Stunning Appliqué Projects Inspired by Turkish Iznik Tiles

Tamsin Harvey

C&T PUBLISHING

Text copyright © 2015 by Tamsin Harvey

Photography and artwork copyright © 2015 by C&T Publishing, Inc.

Publisher: Amy Marson

Creative Director: Gailen Runge

Art Director: Kristy Zacharias

Editor: Lee Jonsson

Technical Editors: Susan Nelsen and Susan Hendrickson

Cover Designer: April Mostek

Book Designer: Christina Jarumay Fox

Production Coordinator: Freesia Pearson Blizard

Production Editor: Katie Van Amburg

Illustrator: Kirstie L. Pettersen

Photo Assistant: Mary Peyton Peppo

Inspirational photography by Tamsin Harvey; Styled photography of projects by Kağan Aybudak; Instructional and subject photography by Diane Pedersen, unless otherwise noted

Published by C&T Publishing, Inc., P.O. Box 1456, Lafayette, CA 94549

Library of Congress Cataloging-in-Publication Data

Harvey, Tamsin, 1978-

Constantinople quilts : 8 stunning appliqué projects inspired by Turkish Iznik tiles / Tamsin Harvey.

pages cm

Includes bibliographical references.

ISBN 978-1-61745-011-2 (soft cover)

1. Quilting--Patterns. 2. Appliqué--Patterns. I. Title.

TT835.H3424 2015

746.46--dc23

2014034185

Printed in China

10 9 8 7 6 5 4 3 2 1

DEDICATION

To Mum and Dad,
who have given me the opportunity,
support, and strength to follow my dreams
and to find my own path in life

ACKNOWLEDGMENTS

When writing a book, you have many people who come on the journey with you. Without their support and encouragement, this book would not have been possible.

Thank you to Angela, for without her help this book and my quilting career would never have occurred.

Thank you to my family and Jan, for allowing me to create and to follow my dreams.

To the staff and extended family at Berrima Patchwork, who have shared this journey with me.

To four amazing mentors, Sandra Leichner, Michele Hill, Mariya Waters, and Carol Doak. You have all encouraged me, supported me, and given me feedback and advice. Thank you for being there when I had no idea what to do, sharing your knowledge and expertise, and so much more. I especially thank you all for your friendships.

To Greg and the staff at Bernina Australia, for the loan of a Bernina 750QE sewing machine and for your encouragement and your belief in my designs.

To Bob and Heather Purcell at Superior Threads, for their friendship and advice. You both do an amazing job of educating consumers about threads and needles. Thank you for the Superior Threads' Kimono silk threads that I had the pleasure of using in the creation of these projects.

To Tim and Jim at Lloyd Curzon Textiles Australia, for their support throughout the process of writing this book and creating the designs.

Thank you to the fantastic team at C&T Publishing, who guided me through the process of writing this book and making it come to life.

To Kağan Aybudak, for the wonderful photographs of the projects, taken on location in Istanbul.

To the team at MA Productions, Münir, Esra, and Yuncay, for sorting out the mountain of paperwork related to the special permits from the mosques, palaces, and museums for the photography and research of this book. Thank you for being my support team and translators while I was in Istanbul.

Also in Turkey, thanks to the following:

Turkish Ministry of Culture and Tourism

Religious Affairs Department of Istanbul Province

Governor's Office of Bursa Province and Istanbul Province

Staff at Rüstem Pasha Mosque

Directorate and staff at Hagia Sophia (Ayasofya) Museum

Directorate and staff at Topkapı Palace Museum and Topkapı Palace Museum Harem Apartments

Directorate and staff at Hotel Arcadia Blue Istanbul

İznik Foundation and Prof. Dr. Işıl Akbaygil

Staff at Sultanahmet Mosque

Staff at Eyüp Sultan Mosque

CONTENTS

Introduction 6

Photo Gallery of the Projects 15

Getting Started 25

How-To Instructions 33

Quiltmaking Basics:
  How to Finish Your Quilt 39

Projects

GELIBOLU BAG 43

SULTAN'S CUSHIONS
  AND BED SCARF 47

NICAEA TABLE RUNNER 53

EYÜP TABLE RUNNER 57

BLUE ÇINI 61

TOPKAPI 66

THE PEACOCK 70

ISTANBUL 74

Supplies and Resources 78

Tile Photo Locations in Istanbul, Turkey ... 78

Bibliography 78

About the Author 79

Introduction

During the sixteenth and seventeenth centuries, the Ottoman Empire was the most powerful state in the world. Because of its location, the Ottoman Empire was at the center of interaction between the Eastern and Western worlds. When the Ottomans conquered various regions, they absorbed many of the traditions, art forms, and institutions of these cultures. They were known for adopting these cultures and then turning their traditions into elaborate new forms, which created a unique and distinctively Ottoman cultural identity.

İznik pottery originated in the town of the same name. İznik is located in western Anatolia, in the province of Bursa, historically known as Nicaea. The town was selected for its nearby deposits of potter's clay and quartz. Trees from a local forest provided the fuel required for the ceramic kilns. İznik's proximity to Constantinople (modern-day Istanbul) allowed for ease of delivery. From the late fifteenth century until the end of the seventeenth century, this town was the main source of ceramics and tiles for the Ottoman Empire.

İznik pottery was originally inspired by Chinese porcelain, highly prized by the Ottoman sultans. While İznik had been creating cheap and rather ordinary pottery since before the fifteenth century, Chinese porcelain was expensive. The Ottoman court began sponsoring a series of workshops that created luxury items worthy of the new court.

The introduction of a new form of ceramic decoration called underglaze painting changed the town into a known source of superb technical quality and artistry. The early examples of İznik wares mainly consisted of one color—cobalt blue.

Cobalt blue tiles from Topkapı Palace

As the artists continued to experiment and develop their trade, they incorporated new colors into their designs. In the 1530s pale purple, green, and turquoise began to be used. With the expanded selection of colors available, more floral motifs emerged, including tulips, carnations, peonies, roses, and hyacinths. İznik wares, prized for their quality and uniqueness, were being exported over much of the Middle East and Europe.

Photos of İznik tiles
located within the tomb
of Sultan Selim II at the
Hagia Sophia Museum

Inside the Sultanahmet Mosque, large İznik tile panels line the walls along the gallery level.

The use of İznik tiles as decoration was slow to emerge. As the artists and new techniques developed, the demand for tile mosaics and panels increased and was stimulated and controlled by court commissions. Examples of these mosaics and panels can still be seen in mosques and palaces throughout Turkey. The Sultanahmet Mosque, located in Istanbul, used more than 20,000 handmade ceramic tiles featuring designs of flowers, fruits, and cypresses, including 50 different tulip designs. It is the tile colors that have given this mosque its more commonly used name of the Blue Mosque.

Stunning panel display found on the gallery level of the Sultanahmet Mosque

One example of the tulip designs found on İznik tiles in the Sultanahmet Mosque

The Topkapı Palace in Istanbul was the primary residence of the Ottoman sultans and their courts from 1465 to 1858. Many rooms, walls, and pavilions within the palace and its grounds feature a selection of tiles, mosaics, and large panels.

One of the many İznik tile-decorated rooms found within the harem at the Topkapı Palace

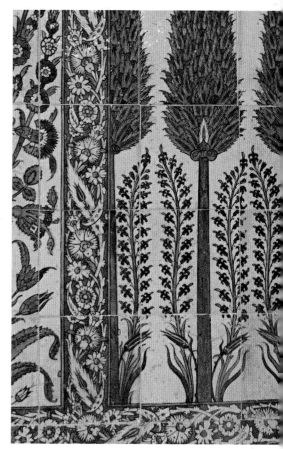

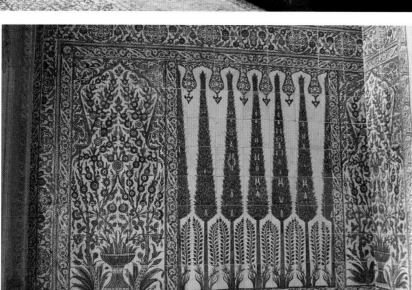

This İznik tile panel found in the harem at the Topkapı Palace was the inspiration for my quilt *Topkapı* (page 66).

Inside the Baghdad kiosk in the Topkapı Palace

İznik tile panels line the walls of the buildings located within the fourth courtyard at the Topkapı Palace.

Several different İznik tile designs line the walls of the summer kiosk at the Topkapı Palace.

The Rüstem Pasha Mosque contains the most spectacular arrangement of İznik tiles found in any mosque. Commissioned by Princess Mihrimah, Süleyman the Magnificent's daughter, in honor of her late husband, Grand Vizier Rüstem Pasha, this mosque was designed by the Ottoman imperial architect Mimar Sinan. Princess Mihrimah wanted to commemorate her late husband with a garden. The interior of the mosque is lined with tiles featuring numerous floral designs, creating an "indoor garden."

Inside the Rüstem Pasha Mosque

The gallery level in the Rüstem Pasha Mosque

İznik tile designs found within the Rüstem Pasha Mosque: This mosque was one of the first to have tiles featuring the coral-red color found within the designs.

The quality of pottery produced in İznik began to decline toward the end of the sixteenth century. With the imposition of fixed prices and a decrease in new imperial building projects, there was little demand for the wares, and the İznik craftsmen could not compete with high-quality imports. During the building of the Sultanahmet Mosque, Sultan Ahmet I forbade all ceramic production in İznik other than that required for the mosque. This led to a decrease in the number of other products being made and a loss of trade for the artists. Many of the artists and craftsmen left İznik during this time, resettling in Kütahya, located in central Turkey. There, they were able to make products such as bowls and plates, which were still in demand.

Today throughout Istanbul and Turkey, the original tiles, panels, and mosaics are on display in palaces, mosques, and tombs. The ceramic wares are highly sought after internationally, and large collections can be viewed in many of the acclaimed museums of the world, including the British Museum in London, the Louvre in Paris, and the Metropolitan Museum of Art in New York City. While cheap imitations of İznik tiles are widely available in the marketplace, The İznik Foundation, located in Istanbul and İznik, Turkey, has spent many years researching the techniques and methods used over 400 years ago and is producing the same high-quality tiles that the artists once created. The foundation is dedicated to educating the world about these prized designs and expanding exposure to them.

Artist at work in the İznik Foundation
Workshop located in İznik, Turkey

PHOTO GALLERY OF
THE PROJECTS

Gelibolu Bag (page 43)

Sultan's Cushion A (page 47)

Sultan's Cushions and Bed Scarf (page 47)

Sultan's Cushion B (page 47)

Nicaea Table Runner (page 53)

Eyüp Table Runner (page 57)

Blue Çini (page 61)

Topkapı (page 66)

The Peacock (page 70)

Istanbul (page 74)

Getting Started

You will need some basic equipment and information before you start one of these projects.

SEWING MACHINE

Many of the projects in this book have been both appliquéd and quilted on a domestic Bernina 750QE sewing machine. Whether you use a new or an old sewing machine, the main feature that is required is a blanket stitch that can be adjusted to different stitch widths and lengths. This is my preferred stitch for appliqué. Many of the newer sewing machines have extra features, which can include an automatic thread cutter, a hover foot, a larger working space between the needle and the motor, a needle up/down feature, and more. These extra features can make machine appliqué easier, and sometimes upgrading to a newer machine is an advantage. Whichever machine you choose, it is important to take care of it. Review the machine manual on how to clean and oil it (as recommended). Have the machine serviced by a licensed mechanic annually, and the machine will appreciate it!

Sewing Machine Feet

For the sewing machine, you will need an open-toe embroidery foot to sew the appliqués. A quarter-inch patchwork foot will provide an accurate ¼" seam allowance when piecing the borders and sewing the projects. A free motion/darning foot and/or walking foot will be required if you are going to machine quilt your projects.

Sewing Machine Stitch

For the project appliqués, I used a blanket stitch. I adjusted my sewing machine to a 1.6-stitch width and a 1.6-stitch length, but remember that your machine may require different settings. On my machine this is a small blanket stitch, which I find "hugs" the appliqué. On some machines this setting may not be available, so I suggest that you play with the adjustment on your machine to achieve the desired stitch size. Before you start stitching on your project, sew a small test piece to give you some practice and allow you to get the feel of the stitch. If you are not happy with the result, try changing the length or width. Test it out and keep changing the settings until you find a suitable stitch setting.

Threads to Use on the Sewing Machine

There are a variety of threads you can use for the project appliqués. When you choose your threads, you must consider whether you want the stitching to be a feature or whether you want it to blend in with the appliqué fabric. For the projects in this book, I selected threads to match the appliqué projects.

For machine-sewn appliqués, I have used Superior Threads' Kimono silk thread. The silk thread is thin and is almost invisible on the appliqué fabric. Being a silk thread, it is strong and has a naturally lustrous sheen. This thread is suitable for sewing machines and can be used for hand stitching as well. Many silks threads are only suitable for hand use, so check before using it on a machine!

A 50- or 40-weight thread is a thicker thread and will stand out on your appliqué. This may be the effect you want to achieve. A polyester thread will provide a shine, while a 100% cotton thread will give a matte appearance.

Sample sewn with 100-weight Kimono silk thread from Superior Threads

Sample sewn with 50-weight 100% cotton thread

Sample sewn with 40-weight 100% polyester thread

Different thread types: A. Superior Threads' 100-weight Kimono silk thread; B. 50-weight 100% cotton thread; C. 40-weight 100% polyester thread

Sewing Machine Tension

Depending on the thread you plan to use, you may need to adjust the tension of the sewing machine. I prefer to use the same thread on the top and in the bobbin. By doing so, I can avoid some of the issues that occur with the tension. Sometimes it is too expensive or not possible to use the same thread. In this situation, I recommend you use your preferred thread on the top and use a bobbin thread in the same color as your top thread. A bobbin fill thread such as Bottom Line by Superior Threads is thinner than general sewing threads and goes a long way toward reducing the amount of time you need to refill the empty bobbin.

If you are using a thin thread as the top thread, anything from a 60-weight upward, you may need to adjust the tension of the machine. With a thinner thread, the tension discs need to be tightened so that the discs will "grip" the thread. If you are using a thick thread as the top thread, anything from a 40-weight and lower, you may need to loosen the tension on the machine to allow the thicker thread to pass through the tension discs without any problems.

Before changing the machine's tension, test a small piece of the base/background fabric along with a piece of the appliqué fabric. It is always important to do a sample using the same fabrics you plan on sewing. Thread the machine with the chosen threads on the top and in the bobbin, and using a blanket stitch, sew several stitches onto the sample. Can you see the bobbin thread on the right side of your appliqué? If you do, you will need to loosen the top tension.

Top thread tension too tight: Loosen top tension. *Note: I used red bobbin thread here to make it easier to see.*

If you can't see any of the bobbin thread, turn your piece of appliqué to the wrong side. Can you see the top thread? If you do, you may need to tighten the top tension.

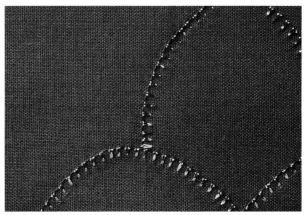

Top thread tension too loose: Tighten top tension. *Note: I used red bobbin thread here to make it easier to see.*

When changing the tension on the sewing machine, review the machine manual for how to do this, and only change it by 0.5 each time. Repeat until the tension is just right.

Sewing-Machine Needles

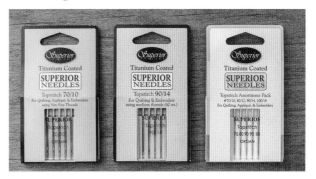

Your choice of sewing-machine needles will depend on your choice of threads. My preference for sewing appliqué and machine quilting are top-stitch needles. They have a large eye, which provides easy threading and won't distort the thread as it passes through the eye. The needles also have a deep groove in which the thread can sit. For thin threads, I suggest using a 70/10 needle. For 50-weight threads, I suggest an 80/12 needle. For thicker threads, anything from a 40-weight thread or lower, a 90/14 needle will be required. Choosing the correct needle size can help you avoid issues with tension, needle breakage, and thread breakage.

HAND-SEWING SUPPLIES

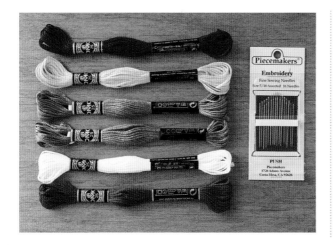

The projects in this book can all be appliquéd by hand. My preferred hand-sewing stitch is the same as that for the sewing machine—a blanket stitch. Stranded embroidery cotton, such as DMC or COSMO thread, is ideal. Choose a thread color that will blend with your appliqué. One or two strands of the thread with your preferred embroidery needle are all that you need for the appliqué.

GENERAL SEWING SUPPLIES

Scissors

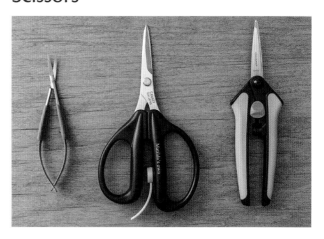

For these projects you will need basic sewing supplies, including a rotary cutter, rotary mat, and ruler; a permanent marker (such as a Sharpie) to clearly mark the design onto the fusible web; and tracing paper. You will also need straight pins for general sewing and safety pins for pinning the three layers before quilting.

Many individual appliqué pieces will be cut for most of the projects. It is best to choose a pair of scissors with a sharp point and thin blades. They must be the right size for your hands and feel comfortable. For larger hands, scissors with big loop handles can be good to use; for smaller hands, scissors with small loop handles may be better. Once the fabric pieces have been appliquéd to the background fabric and sewn into place, you may find that there are some small stray threads. A pair of sharp spring-action scissors, such as EasyKut by ToolTron, is ideal to remove these threads. They are very sharp and snip these threads with ease.

Marking Tools

I cannot stress enough the importance of testing what-ever marking tool you choose on *every* fabric you will be marking to ensure that the marks can be removed. With many different brands of patchwork fabrics on the market, different chemicals and dyes can have varying effects. When you mark your fabric, it may come out easily on one fabric and not another.

■ White pencils or white water-soluble pens are ideal for dark fabrics. When using a water-soluble or iron-off pen, be careful, as sometimes this type of marker can leave a faint residue when removed. Refillable lead pencils, such as the Sewline pencil, come with a range of different color leads. These make it easy to mark different-colored fabrics. Just be careful not to press too hard when using them on the fabric, as that will make it harder to remove your marks. The water-soluble blue marker pens can be useful when marking light fabrics. There are many different varieties on the market. Always choose one from a reputable brand. The Clover fine-point blue marker pens and the Styla blue marker by Sewline have both been used on some of the projects in this book.

■ Chalk pens and markers are some of my favorites, but if you mark a quilt or project with these, you may find that after handling the project too much, the chalk brushes off. Sometimes this is a bonus; however, if you haven't finished and still need those marks, you will have to re-mark them.

Template Interfacing

I trace my patterns onto template interfacing because it is easy to trace on, and it does not shrink when you press it with a cool iron. Bosal's Create-A-Pattern tracing interfacing and Grid It, Grid It from Shades Textiles are both ideal.

For the large appliqué patterns, I trace the designs onto the interfacing material to provide a master copy from which to work. I use these master copies as an overlay or underlay to guide my placement of the appliqués onto the background fabric. Because the template interfacing is lightweight, if you trace a pattern onto one side with a permanent marker, you can see through it on the other side. This means you don't have to reverse the pattern for tracing onto your fusible web or for the layout!

FABRICS

The fabrics chosen to complete the projects in this book are true to the colorings you would find in the İznik ceramics and tiles. Don't let this influence you not to try other colorways for the projects. When choosing the fabrics to use, keep in mind that you don't want large print fabrics unless you plan on fussy cutting them.

For *The Peacock* (page 70), I fussy cut the body feathers from one fabric.

I fussy cut fabric by Timeless Treasures to create individual body feathers in *The Peacock*.

Marble fabrics, such as Maywood Studio's Shadow Play, batiks, a good-quality homespun, or quilter's muslin, and shot cottons all work well for both backgrounds and appliqué. For the backgrounds, select fabrics that are not too busy, or they will distract from the appliqué designs.

Selection of Shadow Play fabrics by Maywood Studio

Selection of premium quilter's homespun from ColorWorks collection by Northcott

For the appliqué flowers and leaves, choose a selection of fabrics with small prints or a tone-on-tone fabric in a range of different colors. Large, busy prints do not work very well.

Ideal fabrics for leaf appliqués

In several of the projects, I used white fabrics. One problem with using a totally white fabric is that if it is used for appliqué, the background fabric can sometimes show through the appliqué or can distort the white color. When choosing white fabrics, find something with a slight print on it. In several of the projects, I used Michael Miller Fabrics' Fairy Frost in the Snow colorway. Although this print is white, there is an overprint of white shimmer, which makes the fabric slightly thicker, ensuring it keeps the white color when used as an appliqué on a dark background.

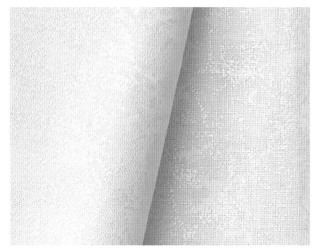

Snow colorway of Fairy Frost by Michael Miller Fabrics

In two of the quilt projects, *Topkapı* (page 66) and *Istanbul* (page 74), I used fabrics from the Pearl Essence collection by Galaxy Fabrics. Once again, these fabrics are white with a silver overprint.

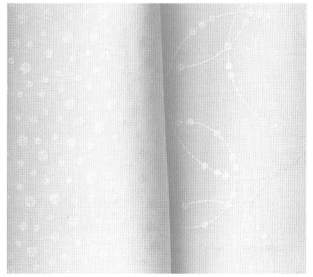

Two different Pearl Essence collection fabrics from Galaxy Fabrics

It is very tempting to use traditional fabrics for these projects; however, think outside the box and use fabrics that have a metallic overprint on them. *The Peacock* has many gold and silver metallic cotton overprint fabrics. They add an interesting dimension to the quilt.

Selection of metallic overprint fabrics ideal for appliqués

BATTING

All the quilts and projects in this book were machine quilted using a blend of wool and polyester batting from the Australian company MiniJumbuk. The blend of batting gives the quilts and projects a puffier look with a faux-trapunto effect, and if they are folded for storage, they tend not to show the creases as much.

I used a thinner cotton batting from Hobbs for the projects I hand quilted, as it allows a needle to pass through with ease. For the bag project, I found that batting created a floppy bag. Instead of batting, I used ByAnnie's Soft and Stable. This product provides the bag with more stability without the need for additional interfacings and gives the bag a more professional finished look.

FUSIBLE WEB

There are several types of fusible web on the market. So which one do you use? A repositionable fusible web like Steam-A-Seam 2 is ideal for the quilts and table runners, which have many appliqué pieces. The pieces can be cut and then placed onto the background fabric. Because it is repositionable, the appliqué pieces can be moved, and the webbing will temporarily stick to the fabric without having to be pressed. Once you have decided on the exact positioning, simply press to fuse.

The only downside to repositionable fusible web is that it is slightly thicker, which makes it difficult to hand stitch, and can leave a residue on the sewing needle. If you are using a sewing machine, there should be no issue.

For a thinner fusible web, SoftFuse from Shades Textiles works well. This fusible web is thin, creating a soft-feeling appliqué. It works well for both machine and hand appliqué and does not leave a "hole" when a needle passes through it.

FABRIC QUANTITIES

When I was writing the requirements for these patterns, I found that some of the appliqués only needed a small amount of fabric. Writing "⅛ yard" just seemed like too much because there would be a large amount left over.

Your stash is always a great place to start when undertaking one of these projects. Some of these projects use several different shades of a particular color. When a project calls for just a small amount of a fabric, you just might have a small piece in your stash that would be perfect.

WORKING IN SECTIONS

For the larger quilts, having a Project Outline Template provides a guide for the appliqué pieces. You can lay out some pieces on the background fabric, fuse, sew, and then go back to place the other appliqué pieces in the correct positions. If the entire quilt is fused at one time, you will find that as the pieces are appliquéd and the project is handled, the unsewn appliqué pieces may start to lift and fray. It is always tempting to fuse the entire quilt in one go; however, consider doing it in parts. This will create a better-looking finished product, and you won't necessarily have the headaches of having to trim all the frayed edges or constantly having to press down the appliqué pieces.

GENERAL INFORMATION

All fabrics used in the projects are at least 42″ wide. A ¼″ seam is used to sew all pieces unless otherwise stated.

I used fusible appliqué in all the projects, and the instructions support this method. Of course, if you want to use another method, such as needle-turn, then be my guest! You will have to add the seam allowance to the appliqué pieces to use that method.

Please enjoy the process of creating these projects. Don't stress too much or overthink the project or process. If you make a mistake, it is okay. Usually you can fix it easily.

How-To Instructions

TRANSFER OF APPLIQUÉ DESIGNS

Creating a Project Outline Template

Locate the appliqué design pattern for your project on the pullout pages. Note that the patterns on the pullout pages have been reversed for tracing onto fusible web.

Check the pattern instructions to see if you will need to trace a guide box or make any layout adjustments. Tape the appliqué pullout page to a flat surface to reduce the page movement. Using a permanent marker, trace the appliqué design onto template interfacing. You are creating a Project Outline Template.

Because the template interfacing is see-through, you can see the markings on both sides, and in some projects you will use both sides of this template in the steps. For these projects you'll see special notes on the pattern. To label the sides for use in those projects, write the labels *Traced Side for Fusible Web* and *Master Copy for Layout* (yes, backward! Or flip the template to the back to write *Master Copy for Layout* the correct way) on your template just as you see it on the pattern page. The steps will reference the Traced Side of your template and the Master Copy side of your template. You can flip the template from one side to the other to read the correct side. Not all project patterns need this label, so if it's not marked on the pattern, don't worry about it!

Trace.

Pattern visible from both sides of template

If pattern has these labels, trace them on your template.

Tracing Designs onto Fusible Web

Trace the appliqué design onto the fusible web. Use the Traced Side of your template or the pullout page. Draw on the paper back of the fusible web with the permanent marker. (Remember that the appliqué designs have been reversed for ease, so you do not need to reverse the pattern for tracing.)

Some projects may use a design element, such as a flower, multiple times. You may wish to trace them together for ease when fusing onto the fabric.

When there are several individual pieces within the same appliqué design, you will need to draw each piece individually.

Some of the appliqué designs overlap. For a piece of appliqué that goes under another piece, draw a dash along the line where these fabrics will meet. Draw an extension of the appliqué design so that it will be tucked under the appliqué design that will appear on top. You will cut the design along this line.

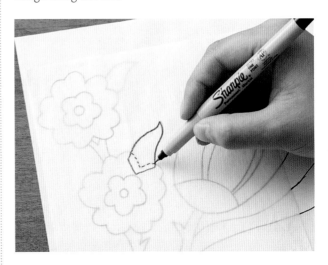

For the larger quilts, it is ideal to number the appliqué pieces as they are traced. This will make it easier to locate the different pieces. As you trace each piece, give it a unique number. Mark this number on the Master Copy side of your Project Outline Template.

Cutting Out and Placing Designs

Once the appliqué designs are traced onto the fusible web, roughly cut out around the designs. If you have traced repetitive design elements and they will be cut from the same fabric, they can be left as a group.

Follow the manufacturer's instructions to fuse the fusible web to the wrong side of the appliqué fabric. Cut around the appliqué designs.

Positioning the Design Using the Template

Take the cut-out appliqué piece and remove the backing paper from the fusible web.

You have the option of placing the Master Copy side of the interfacing either over the background fabric or under the background fabric. If you place it under the background fabric, you may need to use a lightbox.

Master Copy is under background fabric. Lightbox shows design.

When fusing, take note of the order in which the pieces need to be fused. Those pieces that are on the bottom need to be fused first, before fusing other appliqués on top.

With Master Copy under background fabric, place branch and leaf onto background fabric, followed by flower.

If you are using the Master Copy as a guide over the top of the background fabric, layer the appliqué pieces beginning with the bottom layer and building up. Take care when lifting the Master Copy off the background as this can cause the unfused pieces to move slightly.

Place Master Copy on top of background fabric with appliqué positioned underneath so no lightbox is needed.

Remove the Master Copy and press the first appliqué layers into place. Layer and fuse the smaller flower part to the flower base.

Remove Master Copy and fuse appliqués into place.

Fusing Multipiece Flowers

Here's another option for flowers with several layers. Trace the full flower onto the paper side of the fusible web. Trace the small inner pieces separately onto the fusible web.

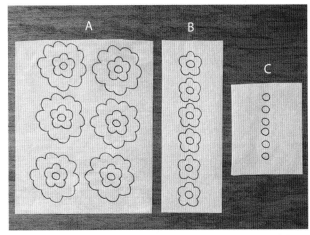

A. Fuse to blue fabric. B. Fuse to yellow fabric. C. Fuse to white fabric.

Fuse the flower parts onto your chosen appliqué fabrics. Cut around the small inner appliqué pieces of the flower. Remove the paper from these small flower pieces.

Place the fused appliqué fabric for the large flower sections on a lightbox with the paper-backing side down. Position the inner flower pieces onto the right side of the appliqué fabric as shown and fuse.

Turn the large flower piece over to the side of the fusible web with the paper still attached. Score around the center of the inner piece with the tip of the scissors. Don't rip or cut through the flower. Remove the fusible paper from this scored center.

Machine stitch to appliqué the inner flower pieces to the large flower piece.

Cut around the outside large flower piece, and remove the fusible paper backing. Position and fuse the flower piece to the background fabric.

MACHINE APPLIQUÉ

Machine Appliqué: Corners

Note: I used a red thread to more clearly show the stitching in these examples.

When approaching the point or corner, slow down and stop 1 stitch before the point, with the needle to the outside of the appliqué.

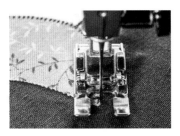

Using the hand wheel on the machine, wind the machine to take 1 stitch, making sure that when the needle goes down, it stops right at the point or corner of the appliqué.

Lift the presser foot with the needle in the down position, and pivot so that the next stitch will swing onto the appliqué fabric piece.

Take the next stitch, and when the needle goes out to the point once again, stop it in the down position. Lift the presser foot and pivot so that the next stitch will be along the edge of the appliqué fabric. Continue sewing.

Machine Appliqué: V Angles

Note: I used a red thread to more clearly show the stitching in these examples.

When approaching the inside V angle, slow down and stop 1 stitch before the angle, with the needle down at the edge of the appliqué fabric.

Using the hand wheel on the machine, wind the machine to take 1 stitch, making sure that when the needle goes down, it stops right in the inside V angle at the edge of the appliqué fabric. Lift the presser foot

with the needle in the down position and pivot.

Needle down at V before pivoting

The next stitch will swing onto the appliqué piece just in from the V angle.

Take the next stitch, and once again stop the needle in the down position when it goes back out to the V angle. Lift the presser foot once again with the needle in the down position, and pivot so that the next stitch is along the edge of the appliqué fabric. Continue sewing.

Quiltmaking Basics:
How to Finish Your Quilt

A ¼" seam allowance is used for all projects unless otherwise stated.

PRESSING THE SEAM ALLOWANCE

For most of the projects, press the seams toward the darker fabrics. Because a great deal of white is used in these quilts, this is very important. Otherwise you may see the darker fabric through the white.

MITERING THE BORDERS

1. If the border is pieced with several strip pieces, sew these pieces together first before joining them to the main quilt. Press.

2. On the quilt center, mark ¼" in from each corner and mark the midpoint of each side. Then mark the midpoint of each border section.

3. Pin the center of the first border strip to the center of the corresponding quilt side. Pin the remainder of the border to the quilt, working from the center to the corners.

4. Sew the border to the side of the quilt top, starting at the ¼" mark at the corner and stopping at the ¼" mark at the end of that side. Backstitch at the start and end to secure the border to the quilt center. The excess length of the side borders will extend beyond each edge.

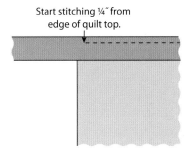

Start stitching ¼" from edge of quilt top.

5. Repeat Steps 1–4 with the other 3 border pieces and quilt sides, remembering to stop and start at the ¼" marks. Press all the seams toward the borders.

6. To create the miter, lay a corner of the quilt top right side up on the ironing board. Lay a border on top of the adjacent border.

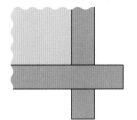

Lay border strip on top of adjacent strip.

7. With right sides up, fold the top border strip under itself so that it meets the edge of the adjacent border and forms a 45° angle. Pin the fold in place.

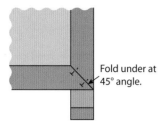

Fold under at 45° angle.

8. Position a 90° angle or ruler over the corner to check that the corner is flat and square. When everything is in place, press the fold firmly.

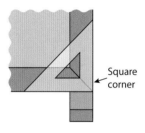

Square corner

9. Remove pins. Fold the center section of the quilt top in half diagonally, right sides together, and align the long edges of the border strips. On the wrong side, place pins near the pressed fold in the corner to secure the border strips.

10. Beginning at the inside corner at the border seamline where the ¼" mark is, stitch, backstitch, and then stitch along the fold toward the outside point of the border corners, being careful not to allow any stretching to occur. Backstitch at the end.

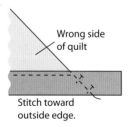

Wrong side of quilt

Stitch toward outside edge.

11. Trim the excess border fabrics to a ¼" seam allowance. Press the seam open.

PINNING THE QUILT

1. Lay out the backing wrong side up, and tape the edges down with masking tape. (If you are working on carpet, you can use T-pins to secure the backing to the carpet.) Center the batting on top, smoothing out any folds.

2. Place the quilt top right side up on top of the batting and backing, making sure it is centered.

3. Baste the quilt. (This keeps the quilt sandwich from shifting while you are quilting.)

■ If you plan to take your quilt to a longarm quilter, you do not have to layer your quilt. Consult with your quilter.

■ If you plan to machine quilt, pin baste the quilt layers together with safety pins placed about 3"–4" apart. Begin basting in the center and move toward the edges, first in vertical, then horizontal rows. Try not to pin directly on the intended quilting lines, and avoid pinning directly into the appliqués, as this can leave small holes. If the appliqué area is large and you need to secure it, place a pin through and then bring it back up in the stitched blanket stitching.

■ If you plan to hand quilt, baste the layers together with thread, using a long needle and light-colored thread. Knot one end of the thread. Making stitches approximately the length of the needle, begin in the center and move out toward the edges in vertical and horizontal rows approximately 4" apart. Add two diagonal rows of basting.

MACHINE QUILTING BASICS

Quilting, whether by hand or machine, enhances the appliqué designs of the quilt. For these quilts and projects, stitching around the appliqué pieces creates depth. You can also echo the appliqué. By heavily quilting these projects, you can create a faux-trapunto effect.

Heavy quilting can create a trapunto effect.

If you are not confident free-motion quilting the in-between spaces and borders of the quilt, consider using patterns from quilting design books or stencils. The feathers in *The Peacock* (page 70) were created using stencils.

Feathers created using stencils

The borders for *Topkapı* (page 66) were also created using a stencil.

Border quilted using feather stencil

BINDING THE QUILT

1. Cut the binding strips 2½″ wide, and piece them together with a diagonal seam to make a continuous binding strip. Trim the seam allowance to ¼″. Press the seams open.

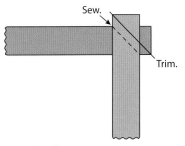

Sew from corner to corner.

Completed diagonal seam

2. Press the entire strip in half lengthwise with wrong sides together. With raw edges even, pin the binding to the front edge of the quilt a few inches away from the corner, and leave the first few inches of binding unattached. Start sewing, using a ¼" seam allowance. Stop ¼" away from the first corner and backstitch 1 stitch. Lift the presser foot and needle.

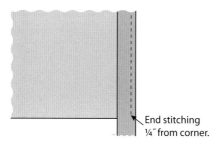

End stitching
¼" from corner.

3. Rotate the quilt ¼ turn. Fold the binding at a right angle so it extends straight above the quilt and the fold forms a 45° angle in the corner. Then bring the binding strip down even with the edge of the quilt. Begin sewing at the folded edge. Repeat this step for all corners. Continue stitching until you are back near the beginning of the binding strip.

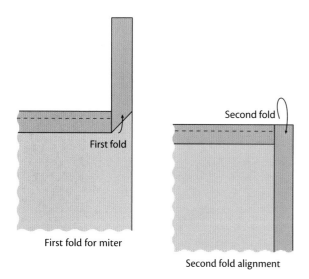

First fold

First fold for miter

Second fold

Second fold alignment

4. To finish the binding ends, fold the ending tail of the binding back on itself where it meets the beginning binding tail. From the fold, measure and mark the cut width of your binding strip. Cut the ending binding tail to this measurement. For example, if your binding is cut 2½" wide, measure from the fold on the ending tail of the binding 2½", and cut the binding tail to this length.

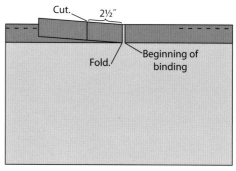

Cut.   2½"

Fold.   Beginning of binding

Cut binding tail.

5. Open both tails. Place one tail on top of the other tail at right angles, right sides together. Mark a diagonal line from corner to corner, and stitch the line. Check that you've done it correctly and that the binding fits the quilt; then trim the seam allowance to ¼". Press the seam open.

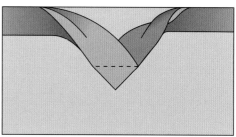

Stitch ends on binding diagonally.

6. Refold the binding, and stitch this binding section in place on the quilt. Fold the binding over the raw edges to the quilt back, and hand stitch in place.

GELIBOLU BAG

FINISHED SIZE:
15″ × 13½″ × 1½″
(38cm × 34cm × 4cm)

Gelibolu is the name of a town and a district in the Çanakkale Province, located in Turkish Thrace. This town is also known as Gallipoli. Gallipoli has a very strong link with Australia, because during the First World War it was the location of a series of memorable battles, including the first major involvement of the Australian and New Zealand Army Corps (ANZAC). This campaign was regarded as the greatest Ottoman victory during the First World War and was considered a major Allied failure. The Allied and Turkish forces both suffered heavy casualties; over 11,000 ANZACs were killed and 33,500 injured. The events that took place in the First World War played a major role in the movement toward the Turkish War of Independence and led to the founding of the Republic of Turkey under the leadership of Mustafa Kemal Atatürk. Atatürk had been a Turkish commander during the Gallipoli campaign. He led the Turkish National Movement in the Turkish War of Independence and became the first president of the Republic of Turkey in 1923.

In 1934, Atatürk wrote a tribute to the ANZACs killed at Gallipoli:

Those heroes that shed their blood and lost their lives… You are now lying in the soil of a friendly country. Therefore rest in peace. There is no difference between the Johnnies and the Mehmets to us where they lie side by side now here in this country of ours… You, the mothers, who sent their sons from faraway countries, wipe away your tears; your sons are now lying in our bosom and are in peace. After having lost their lives on this land they have become our sons as well.

April 25, 2015, marks the 100-year anniversary of the ANZAC's involvement in the Gallipoli Campaign.

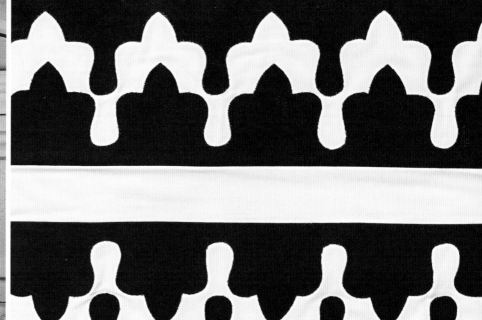

MATERIALS

Yardage is based on 42"-wide fabric.

- **Feature fabric:** 1 yard (92cm) for bag

- **Lining:** ⅝ yard (58cm)

- **White:** ⅓ yard (31cm) for accent

- **Batting:** 40″ × 40″ (102cm × 102cm), either fusible or nonfusible (I used ByAnnie's Soft and Stable.)

- **Fusible web:** 2 pieces 6″ × 18″ (15cm × 46cm)

- **Permanent marker (such as a Sharpie) or pencil:** to mark fusible web and template

- **Template interfacing**

- **Threads for appliqué**

- **Blank CD** or something of similar shape

CUTTING

All measurements include ¼" seam allowances.

FEATURE FABRIC

- Cut 1 strip 14″ × width of fabric; subcut 1 piece 14″ × 15½″ and 2 pieces 7″ × 20″.

- Cut 1 strip 6″ × width of fabric; subcut 2 pieces 6″ × 18″.

- Cut 4 strips 2½″ × width of fabric; subcut 2 pieces 2½″ × 40″ and 4 pieces 2½″ × 20″.

LINING

- Cut 1 strip 14″ × width of fabric; subcut 2 pieces 14″ × 15½″.

- Cut 2 strips 2½″ × width of fabric; subcut 2 strips 2½″ × 40″.

WHITE

- Cut 1 strip 6½″ × width of fabric; subcut 2 pieces 6½″ × 18″.

- Cut 1 strip 2″ × width of fabric; subcut 1 piece 2″ × 15½″.

BATTING

- Cut 2 pieces 14″ × 15½″.

- Cut 2 pieces 2½″ × 20″.

- Cut 2 pieces 2½″ × 40″.

PREPARATION

Refer to How-To Instructions (pages 33–38) as needed.

1. Locate the *Gelibolu Bag* appliqué pattern on pullout page P4. Refer to Creating a Project Outline Template (page 33) to make the template for your project. Trace the pattern onto your template interfacing, using a permanent marker. You do not have to mark this template as Traced Side or Master Copy side, because the pattern is symmetrical and does not create a mirror image when turned from one side to another. You can trace from either side of the template.

2. Refer to Tracing Designs onto Fusible Web (page 34). Position the template so it's centered on the paper side of a 6″ × 18″ piece of fusible web. Trace the template for the appliqué onto each piece of fusible web, using a permanent marker or pencil. When tracing, be sure to trace the box outline on the fusible web as well. Leave approximately ½″ beyond this box when trimming off any excess fusible web.

3. Following the manufacturer's directions, fuse the web onto the wrong side of each feature fabric 6″ × 18″ piece. Then cut along the long straight top and bottom lines of the template (not the short ends yet). Do not remove the paper backing yet.

4. Carefully cut along the center appliqué line of a feature fabric fused piece. Both pieces of this fused fabric will be used, so you must cut exactly on the indicated line. Be extra careful not to make a mistake or cut away too much. Do not cut the ends of the box just yet; leave the excess at the ends. Keep these 2 pieces together as a set. Repeat this step to cut the other feature fabric fused piece, and keep the 2 pieces as a separate set.

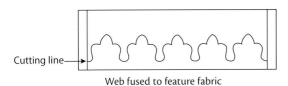

Cutting line →

Web fused to feature fabric

5. Keeping the appliqué pieces in sets, mark the center point on the long straight fabric edge of each piece of the sets.

6. Mark the center point on the long edges of both white 6½″ × 18″ pieces.

7. Remove the paper backing from 1 appliqué set. Line up the long straight edge of 1 appliqué piece on the bottom edge of a white 6½″ × 18″ piece, matching the center points. Then line up the remaining appliqué piece from the set with the top edge on the same white piece, matching the center points. There will be excess fabric at the ends of the appliqués. Fuse into place.

8. Repeat Step 7 with the remaining appliqué set and white 6½″ × 18″ piece to give a total of 2 appliqué panels.

APPLIQUÉ

Refer to Machine Appliqué (page 38) as needed.

Use your preferred method to appliqué the curved lines that were the center cut lines of the appliqués. Use thread to match your feature fabric. You do not need to appliqué the straight edges of the appliqués.

CONSTRUCTION

Seam allowances are ¼″ unless otherwise noted.

Refer to How-To Instructions (pages 33–38) as needed.

1. Trim the width of the appliqué panels to 15½″, measuring 7¾″ from the center in each direction.

2. Refer to the project photo (page 43) for the correct orientation of the appliqué panels, and sew the white 2″ × 15½″ strip between the 2 appliqué panels. Press the seams away from the white strip.

3. Fuse or tack a batting 14″ × 15½″ piece to the wrong side of the pieced bag front.

4. Fuse or tack the other batting 14″ × 15½″ piece to the wrong side of the feature fabric 14″ × 15½″ piece for the bag back.

5. Sew the 2 feature fabric 2½″ × 40″ strips together end to end. Fuse or tack the 2 batting 2½″ × 40″ strips to the long feature fabric strip to create the bag's gusset piece. Trim any excess batting, and set this aside for now.

6. Lay the bag's front piece with batting on a flat surface. Trace the curve of the CD on the lower corners of the bag front as shown, and cut the curved corners. Repeat this on the bag back piece with fleece and the 2 lining 15½″ × 14″ pieces.

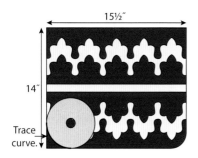

7. For the pockets of the bag, fold each feature fabric 7″ × 20″ piece in half, right sides together, so that the folded strip measures 7″ × 10″. Sew along the edges with a ¼″ seam, leaving a small opening so you can turn the pockets right side out. Turn right side out and press.

8. Measure 4″ from the lower edge of the lining 15½″ × 14″ piece. Center a pocket on the piece at this line, and pin the pocket in place as shown,

ensuring the turn opening is on the bottom so it will be stitched shut as the pocket is stitched to the lining. Stitch into place along the edge of the pocket as shown. Stitch down the center of the pocket, if desired, to create 2 smaller pockets. Repeat with the other pocket and lining fabric.

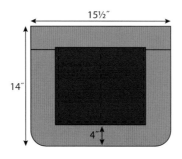

9. Pin the bag's front piece and the gusset piece right sides together, with the gusset strip seam centered at the bottom of the bag front. Make sure that it is pinned well around the curves. Sew together using a ¼″ seam. The gusset piece is very long, so trim the ends even with the bag front after the pieces are sewn together.

10. With right sides together, pin the bag's back piece to the gusset/front piece of the bag. Sew together.

11. Repeat Steps 9 and 10 with the lining 14″ × 15½″ pieces and the lining 2½″ × 40″ piece. However, leave a 3″ opening in 1 of the seams to allow the bag to be turned right side out in the final step. Trim the gusset as needed. Do not turn the lining right side out.

12. To make a bag handle, layer 2 feature fabric 2½″ × 20″ pieces

right sides together. Layer a batting 2½″ × 20″ piece on the bottom as shown.

13. Sew the bag handle together using a ¼″ seam along the 2 long edges. Turn right side out, press flat, and topstitch the 2 long edges ¼″ from the edges. Repeat to make a second handle.

14. To sew the first handle to the bag, find the top center of the bag back and mark 2″ on either side of the center. Align the edge of the handle on the 2″ mark, with the raw top edge on the outside of the bag. Baste the handle in place. Repeat with the other handle on the bag front.

15. Place the outside of the bag into the lining and pin, right sides together. Stitch around the top of the bag. Turn the bag right side out through the opening left in the lining fabric.

16. Press the top of the bag flat, and topstitch ¼″ around the top of the bag. Stitch the opening in the lining closed where you turned the bag.

SULTAN'S CUSHIONS
AND BED SCARF

Cushions and Bed Scarf hand appliquéd and hand quilted by Angela Perry. Fabrics featured in these projects are from the ColorWorks collection by Northcott.

FINISHED SIZE:
Cushions, 24″ × 24″
        (61cm × 61cm)
Bed Scarf, 16″ × 100½″
        (41cm × 255cm)

The sultans of the Ottoman dynasty ruled the Ottoman Empire from 1299 to 1922. The Ottoman sultan was the absolute ruler of the territory, and his words were law. A total of 36 sultans ruled during the Ottoman dynasty. This empire was one of the most powerful states in the world. In the seventeenth century, it contained 32 provinces. The location of the Ottoman capital of Constantinople (modern-day Istanbul) was ideal, at the center of trade between Europe and Asia on the Mediterranean Basin.

Yardage is based on 42"-wide fabric.

Cushion A

- **Blue:** 1¾ yards (160cm) for front, back, and appliqués
- **White:** ⅓ yard (23cm) for front

- **Red:** ⅛ yard (12cm) or small scraps for flowers
- **Aqua:** ⅛ yard (12cm) or small scraps for flowers
- **Light solid:** 26″ × 26″ (66cm × 66cm) for quilt backing of cushion front
- **Batting:** 26″ × 26″ (66cm × 66cm)
- **Fusible web:** ½ yard (46cm) of 18″ wide (46cm)
- **Permanent marker (such as a Sharpie) or pencil:** to mark fusible web and template

- **Iron-off pen or pencil:** to mark fabric
- **Template interfacing**
- **Threads for appliqué**
- **Thread for quilting**
- **Spray starch**
- **European cushion insert:** 24″ × 24″ (61cm × 61cm)
- **¾″ Clover bias maker** *(optional)*

Cushion B

- **Blue:** 1¾ yards (160cm) for cushion front, back, and appliqués

- **White:** ½ yard (46cm)
- **Red:** ⅛ yard (10cm) or small scraps for flowers
- **Aqua:** ⅛ yard (10cm) or small scraps for flowers
- **Light solid:** 26″ × 26″ (66cm × 66cm) for quilt backing of cushion front
- **Batting:** 26″ × 26″ (66cm × 66cm)
- **Fusible web:** ½ yard (46cm) of 18″ wide (46cm)
- **Permanent marker (such as a Sharpie) or pencil:** to mark fusible web and template

- **Iron-off pen or pencil:** to mark fabric
- **Template interfacing**
- **Threads for appliqué**
- **Thread for quilting**
- **Spray starch**
- **European cushion insert:** 24″ × 24″ (61cm × 61cm)
- **¾″ Clover bias maker** *(optional)*

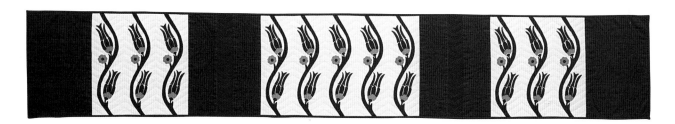

Bed Scarf

- **Blue:** 1¼ yards (115cm) for scarf and appliqués

- **White:** 1 yard (92cm) for scarf

- **Red:** ⅓ yard (30cm) for appliqués

- **Aqua:** ⅛ yard (10cm) for appliqués

- **Fusible web:** 1½ yards (138cm) of 18″ wide (46cm)

- **Backing:** 24″ (61cm) × 106″ (270cm)

- **Binding:** ½ yard (46cm)

- **Batting:** 24″ (61cm) × 106″ (270cm)

- **Permanent marker (such as a Sharpie) or pencil:** to mark fusible web and template

- **Iron-off pen or pencil:** to mark fabric

- **Template interfacing**

- **Threads for appliqué**

- **Thread for quilting**

CUTTING

All measurements include ¼″ seam allowances.

Cushion A

WHITE
- Cut 1 piece 5½″ × 24½″.

BLUE
- Cut 2 strips 24½″ × width of fabric; subcut 1 piece 15½″ × 24½″, 2 pieces 12½″ × 24½″, 2 pieces 6½″ × 24½″, and 1 piece 5½″ × 24½″.

- Cut 3 strips 1½″ × width of fabric; subcut 6 strips 1½″ × 18″.

Cushion B

WHITE
- Cut 2 pieces 5½″ × 24½″.

BLUE
- Cut 2 strips 24½″ × width of fabric; subcut 2 pieces 12½″ × 24½″, 2 pieces 6½″ × 24½″, 1 piece 5½″ × 24½″, and 2 pieces 5″ × 24½″.

- Cut 3 strips 1½″ × width of fabric; subcut 6 strips 1½″ × 18″.

Bed Scarf

WHITE
- Cut 2 strips 16½″ × width of fabric; subcut 1 piece 16½″ × 25½″ and 2 pieces 15½″ × 16½″.

BLUE
- Cut 2 strips 16½″ × width of fabric; subcut 2 pieces 10½″ × 16½″ and 4 pieces 5½″ × 16½″.

RED
- Cut 1 strip 3″ × width of fabric; subcut 2 pieces 3″ × 16½″.

BINDING
- Cut 6 strips 2½″ × width of fabric.

PREPARATION

Refer to How-To Instructions (pages 33–38) as needed.

For Cushion A, Cushion B, and the Bed Scarf

1. Locate the *Sultan's Cushions and Bed Scarf* appliqué patterns on pullout page P3. Refer to Creating a Project Outline Template (page 33) to make the template for your project. Trace the pattern onto your template interfacing, using a permanent marker. Follow the instructions on the pattern to copy the design section needed for Cushions A and B or for the Bed Scarf. Be sure to trace the labels *Traced Side for Fusible Web* and *Master Copy for Layout* (backward) on your template.

2. Refer to Tracing Designs onto Fusible Web (page 34). Using the Traced Side of the template, trace the appliqué designs onto the paper side of the fusible web, using a permanent marker. For Cushion A, trace 1 set of design elements. For Cushion B, trace 2 sets of design elements. For the Bed Scarf, trace 11 sets of design elements.

3. Roughly cut around each of the traced appliqué designs, and divide them into piles to correspond with their chosen fabrics. Follow the manufacturer's directions to fuse the fusible web onto the wrong side of the chosen fabrics.

4. Cut out all the design elements. Remove the paper backing.

CONSTRUCTION

Refer to How-To Instructions (pages 33–38) as needed.

Placing and Fusing the Appliqué Pieces

FOR CUSHIONS A AND B

1. Place the Master Copy side of your template even with the ends and centered on a white 5½" × 24½" piece to position the appliqué pieces.

2. Once you are happy with the placement of all the appliqués, follow the manufacturer's instructions to fuse them into place.

3. Complete 1 appliqué panel for Cushion A and 2 appliqué panels for Cushion B.

FOR THE BED SCARF

1. Both white 15½" × 16½" pieces will have 3 repeats of the appliqué design. To evenly space these designs across the white fabric, use an iron-off pen to mark a line ¼" in from each 16½" side. From these lines, mark lines 5" apart as shown. The marks are guidelines for placing the appliqués.

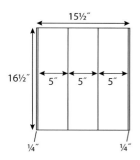

2. Using the Master Copy side of your template as the layout guide, position the appliqué pieces within the guidelines of 1 section of the white fabric.

3. Once you are happy with the placement of the appliqué pieces in 1 section, follow the manufacturer's instructions to fuse them into place.

4. Repeat Steps 2 and 3 to complete 3 appliqué sections on each white 15½" × 16½" piece. Refer to the project photo (page 49) to note the direction of the appliqué sections.

5. The white 25½" × 16½" piece will have 5 repeats of the appliqué design. To evenly space these designs across this white piece, use an iron-off pen to mark a line ¼" in from each 16½" side. From these lines, mark lines 5" apart as shown.

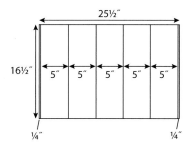

6. Using the Master Copy side of your template as the layout guide, position the appliqué pieces within the guidelines of 1 section of the white fabric.

7. Once you are happy with the placement of all the appliqué pieces in 1 section, follow the manufacturer's instructions to fuse them into place.

8. Refer to the project photo (page 49) to note the direction of the appliqué sections. Repeat Steps 6 and 7 to complete 5 sections on the white 25½" × 16½" piece.

Appliqué for All Projects

Refer to How-To Instructions (pages 33–38) as needed.

Use your preferred method to appliqué around each of the appliqué pieces on your project.

Assembly

FOR CUSHION A

1. Sew the appliqué panel between the blue 15½" × 24½" piece and the blue 5½" × 24½" piece. Press the seams toward the blue.

2. Layer and pin the cushion front with the batting and light-color solid backing, and quilt as desired.

3. Trim the quilted pillow front to 24½" × 24½".

FOR CUSHION B

1. Refer to the Cushion B project photo (page 48) to note the direction of the appliqué panels. Sew the blue 5½" × 24½" piece between the 2 appliqué panels. Press the seams toward the blue.

2. Sew a blue 5" × 24½" piece on the outside of each appliqué panel to complete the cushion front. Press the seams toward the blue.

3. Layer and pin the cushion front with the batting and light-color solid backing, and quilt as desired.

4. Trim the quilted pillow front to 24½" × 24½".

FOR THE BACK OF CUSHIONS A AND B

1. Lightly spray-starch each of the 6 blue 1½" × 18" strips. Press each strip in half lengthwise. Open the strip and press the outside edges to meet at the center crease with wrong sides together. Then repress the original center fold. (You can use the optional bias maker to fold the strips.)

2. With the strips still folded, top-stitch along each side of the folded strip. At 1 end of each strip, turn the raw edge under itself and stitch so that you cannot see the raw edge, or simply tie a knot and trim any excess fabric. These are the cushion tie strips.

3. Lay a blue 12½" × 24½" piece on your table, right side up. Mark the center point and 6" on either side of the center. Use 3 tie strips. Place the raw edge of a tie strip at each mark point as shown, and tack the ties in place. *(Note: The tie strips are white for visual purposes in the illustration.)*

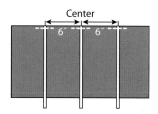

4. Fold a blue 6½" × 24½" piece in half lengthwise with right sides out. Place this on the unit from Step 2, lining up the raw edges as shown. Sew together. Do not press yet.

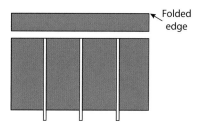

5. Repeat Steps 3 and 4 to make another unit.

6. Take 1 of the sewn backing units from Steps 3 and 4, and flip the 3″ section to the back with the ties pulled straight up as shown. Press the seam toward the larger section. Topstitch along the seamline as shown.

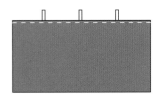

7. Press the seam toward the smaller section on the other backing unit as shown.

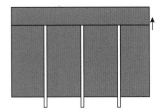

8. Layer the cushion in the following order: front of the cushion appliqué side up, the topstitched backing unit from Step 6 wrong side up on the left side of the cushion front, and the backing unit from Step 7 wrong side up on the right side of the cushion front as shown.

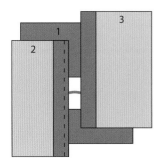

9. With the edges evenly aligned, stitch around all the edges. Sew the raw edges with a zigzag stitch, or serge them to prevent fraying. Turn the cushion right side out and put in the pillow insert. Tie the cushion back closed.

For the Bed Scarf

1. Using the scarf layout diagram, position the 3 appliqué panels, 2 blue 10½″ × 16½″ pieces, 4 blue 5½″ × 16½″ pieces, and 2 red 3″ × 16½″ pieces as shown. Refer to the project photo (page 49) and the diagram to note the direction of the appliqué panels.

2. Sew the scarf together, and press the seams toward the blue.

3. Layer the scarf with the batting and backing. Quilt as desired.

4. Use the binding 2½″ strips to finish the scarf.

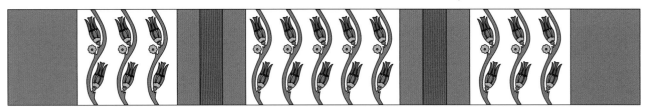

Scarf layout

NICAEA TABLE RUNNER

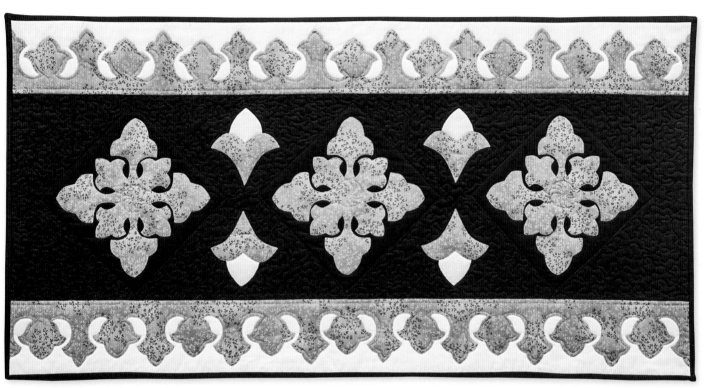

FINISHED SIZE:
40″ × 20″
(102cm × 51cm)

Nicaea is the ancient city now known as İznik, located only a few hours from Istanbul. Throughout history it has been an important town, hosting the First Council of Nicaea by Roman Emperor Constantine I in AD 325 and the Second Council of Nicaea, which are regarded as the first and seventh ecumenical councils in the early history of the Christian church. It was the interim capital city of the Byzantine Empire between 1204 and 1261. The fall of Constantinople in 1453 resulted in the town losing importance until the fifteenth and sixteenth centuries, when it became the center for ceramic creations.

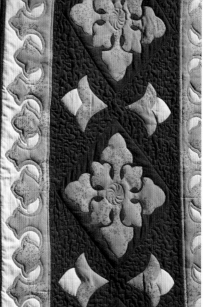

MATERIALS

Yardage is based on 42"-wide fabric.

- **Light blue:** ⅞ yard (70cm) for appliqués

- **White:** ½ yard (45cm) for border and appliqués

- **Dark blue:** ⅜ yard (35cm) for background

- **Backing:** ¾ yard (55cm)

- **Binding:** ⅜ yard (35cm)

- **Batting:** 24″ × 44″ (61cm × 112cm)

- **Fusible web:** 48″ (122cm) of 18″ wide (46cm)

- **Permanent marker (such as a Sharpie) or pencil:** to mark fusible web and template

- **Iron-off pen or pencil:** to mark fabric

- **Template interfacing**

- **Threads for appliqué**

- **Thread for machine quilting**

CUTTING

All measurements include ¼″ seam allowances.

LIGHT BLUE
- Cut 2 strips 4″ × 41″.
- Cut 3 squares 10″ × 10″.
- Cut 4 squares 5″ × 5″.

WHITE
- Cut 2 strips 4½″ × 41″.
- Cut 4 squares 2½″ × 2½″.

DARK BLUE
- Cut 1 strip 12″ × 40″.

BINDING
- Cut 4 strips 2½″ × width of fabric.

FUSIBLE WEB
- Cut 2 strips 4″ × 41″.

PREPARATION

Refer to How-To Instructions (pages 33–38) as needed.

1. Locate the *Nicaea Table Runner* A, B, C, and border appliqué patterns on pullout page P3. Refer to Creating a Project Outline Template (page 33) to make the templates for your project. Trace the patterns onto your template interfacing, using a permanent marker. When you trace the border pattern, also trace the box onto the interfacing. You do not have to mark this template as Traced Side or Master Copy side, because the pattern is symmetrical and does not create a mirror image when turned from one side to another. You can trace from either side of the template.

2. Refer to Tracing Designs onto Fusible Web (page 34). Trace the A, B, and C templates onto the paper side of the remaining fusible web, using a permanent marker or pencil. Trace template A 3 times, template B 4 times, and template C 4 times. Roughly cut around each of the traced A, B, and C appliqué elements. The border template will be traced in Step 5.

3. Following the manufacturer's directions, position the fusible web onto the wrong side of the fabric as indicated:

- Fuse the A pieces to the 3 light blue 10″ × 10″ squares.
- Fuse the B pieces to the 4 light blue 5″ × 5″ squares.
- Fuse the C pieces to the 4 white 2½″ × 2½″ squares.
- Cut all the designs on the traced lines.

4. Mark the center point on the length of each fusible web 4″ × 41″ strip.

5. Align the center of the border template with the center of a fusible strip. Trace the border template without drawing vertical lines at either end. Realign the template to the left to continue the pattern, and trace again, this time drawing a vertical line at the left end of the template. Realign the template to the right of the original tracing, and trace, drawing a vertical line on the right end. Do not trim the ends of the fusible strip beyond the tracing. Repeat with the second strip of fusible web.

6. Following the manufacturer's directions, position the fusible web onto the wrong side of the light blue 4″ × 41″ strip and fuse. Repeat for the second border piece. Cut out borders on the center traced lines, but do not trim the ends of the border pieces. You will only use the wider section of each strip, so set aside or discard the narrower border strip. Remove the paper backing.

CONSTRUCTION

Refer to How-To Instructions (pages 33–38) as needed.

Placing and Fusing the Appliqué Pieces

1. Using an iron-off pen or pencil, mark lines on the vertical and horizontal centers of the dark blue 12″ × 40″ strip as shown.

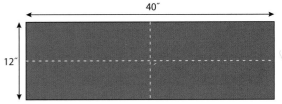

Mark horizontal and vertical centers.

2. From the center vertical line, measure and mark 4 more vertical lines at 6″ intervals as shown.

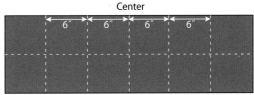

Mark additional vertical lines.

3. On the 2 lines 6″ from the center, measure ¾″ from the top and bottom edges of the fabric, and draw short lines as shown. Measure ¾″ above and below the center horizontal line on the same lines, and draw short lines ¾″ as shown. Be sure to use an iron-off marking pen or pencil.

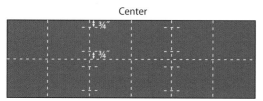

Center

Add additional guidelines.

4. Remove the backing paper from the fusible web on the A, B, and C pieces. Refer to the project photo (page 53) to position the appliqués on the dark blue background as follows:

■ Place the white C pieces on the vertical lines marked in Step 3. The round edge of C rests on the ¾″ marks in from the outside edges as shown. Follow the manufacturer's instructions to fuse these pieces in place.

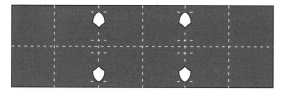

■ Place the light blue B pieces just overlapping the C pieces with the bottom tips resting on the marks that are ¾″ from the center horizontal line as shown. Fuse these pieces in place.

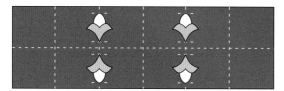

■ Place the light blue A pieces over the intersections of the remaining horizontal and vertical lines, using the lines as guides to ensure that the points of the A pieces are on these lines. Fuse these pieces in place.

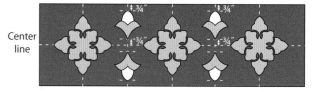

Center line

5. Place a light blue fused border piece on top of a white 4½″ × 41″ strip, lining up the bottom edges carefully. Fuse in place. Repeat to make a second border section. Refer to the project photo (page 53) to see the borders.

Appliqué

Refer to Machine Appliqué (page 38) as needed.

Use your preferred method to appliqué around each of the pieces.

Borders

1. Trim the length of the borders to 40″, measuring 20″ from the center of each strip.

2. Refer to the project photo (page 53) for the correct orientation of the borders to the center panel. Pin the borders to the dark blue appliqué panel, with the light blue and dark blue right sides together.

3. Sew on the borders, using a ¼″ seam allowance. Press the seams toward the center.

Finishing

1. Layer the table runner top, batting, and backing. Quilt as desired.

2. Use the binding 2½″ strips to finish your table runner.

EYÜP TABLE RUNNER

FINISHED SIZE:
18″ × 45″
(46cm × 114cm)

Located in the area of Istanbul, Eyüp is on the Golden Horn, and the region extends to the Black Sea. The town itself lies beyond the walls of Istanbul and is known as a burial area. The Eyüp Sultan Mosque is a sacred place, as it holds the remains of Abu Ayyub al-Ansari, the companion and standard-bearer of the Prophet Muhammad. As part of the Arab Army, al-Ansari was killed during the first attempt to capture Constantinople and was buried here. This table runner is based on an İznik tile that can be found in the Eyüp Sultan Mosque.

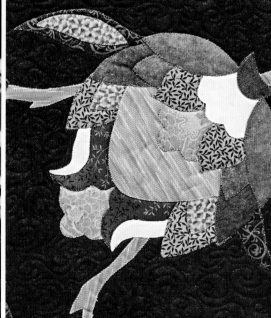

MATERIALS

Yardage is based on 42"-wide fabric.

- **Red:** 1⅜ yards (126cm) for background and backing

- **White:** ¼ yard (20cm) for appliqués

- **Dark blue:** ¼ yard (20cm) for appliqués

- **Light blue:** ¼ yard (20cm) for appliqués

- **Gold:** ⅛ yard (15cm) for appliqués

- **Green:** assortment of scraps (I used 7 different green fabrics in a range of tones.)

- **Binding:** ⅜ yard (35cm) binding

- **Batting:** 22" × 49" (56cm × 125cm)

- **Fusible web:** ¾ yard (69cm) × 18" wide (46cm)

- **Permanent marker (such as a Sharpie) or pencil:** to mark fusible web and template

- **Iron-off pen or pencil:** to mark fabric

- **Template interfacing**

- **Threads for appliqué**

- **Thread for machine quilting**

CUTTING

All measurements include ¼" seam allowances.

RED
- Cut 2 pieces 20" × 48".

BINDING
- Cut 4 strips 2½" × width of fabric.

PREPARATION

Refer to How-To Instructions (pages 33–38) as needed.

1. Locate the *Eyüp Table Runner* pattern on pullout page P3. Refer to Creating a Project Outline Template (page 33) to make the template for your project. On the template interfacing, use a permanent pen to mark a box that is 18″ × 45″ in size. Mark the center of this box with a dashed horizontal line and a dashed vertical line as shown.

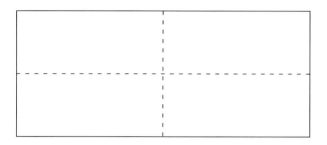

2. Position the pattern with the circle flower in line with the center lines of your template interfacing, and line up the edge of the box on the pattern with the lines you have marked on the template. Trace the pattern, completely tracing the center flower.

3. To complete the other half of the template, rotate the pattern 180° and align the box on the pattern with the lines you have marked on the template. The center flower will not align with the rotated pattern, but that's okay. Trace the remainder of the pattern. Be sure to also trace the labels *Traced Side for Fusible Web* and *Master Copy for Layout* (backward) on your template.

4. Refer to Tracing Designs onto Fusible Web (page 34). Using the Traced Side of the template, trace the appliqué designs onto the paper side of the fusible web using a permanent marker or pencil.

5. Cut around each of the traced appliqué designs roughly, and divide them into piles to correspond with their chosen fabrics. Follow the manufacturer's directions to fuse the fusible web onto the wrong side of the fabric.

6. Cut all the appliqué pieces on the traced lines, and remove the paper backing.

CONSTRUCTION

Refer to How-To Instructions (pages 33–38) as needed.

Placing and Fusing the Appliqué Pieces

1. On a red 20″ × 49″ piece, use an iron-off pen or pencil to draw a box 18″ × 45″ in the center of the fabric. Mark the center of the fabric with dashed lines along the horizontal and vertical centers as you did on the template.

2. Refer to Positioning the Design Using the Template (page 35) and Fusing Multipiece Flowers (page 36). Using the Master Copy side of the template, place the appliqué cutouts onto the background fabric.

3. Follow the manufacturer's instructions to fuse your appliqué pieces into place.

Appliqué

Refer to Machine Appliqué (page 38) as needed.

Use your preferred method to appliqué around each of the pieces.

Finishing

1. Layer the appliquéd top, batting, and backing. Quilt the table runner as desired.

2. Once quilted, trim the table runner on the lines of the marked box (18″ × 45″).

3. Use the binding 2½″ strips to finish the table runner.

BLUE ÇINI

Hand appliquéd and hand quilted by Angela Perry

FINISHED SIZE:
58″ × 58″
(147cm × 147cm)

This was one of the first quilts I created for this book and, as an homage, I named it *Blue Çini*. *Çini* translates from the Turkish as "china." The early examples of İznik wares mainly consisted of two colors—cobalt blue and white. As the skills of the artists developed, they used more colors and varied designs to create the İznik tiles. Many of the first tiles created in İznik were heavily influenced by Chinese porcelain and were a blend of these elements and arabesque patterns. The center star is influenced by the Seljuq tile designs, which predated the İznik tile designs.

MATERIALS

Yardage is based on 42"-wide fabric.

- **White:** 2⅔ yards (245cm) for background and appliqués

- **Dark blue:** 1⅔ yards (150cm) for inside border and appliqués

- **Pale blue:** ⅔ yard (60cm) for appliqués

- **Light blue:** ½ yard (45cm) for appliqués

- **Royal blue:** ½ yard (30cm) for appliqués

- **Binding:** ½ yard (45cm)

- **Backing:** 3⅝ yards (320cm)

- **Batting:** 64" × 64" (160cm × 160cm)

- **Fusible web:** 5 yards (4.6m) of 18" wide (46cm). If you can obtain wider fusible web, that would be an advantage because the center design is 30" square; otherwise, you will need to join the fusible web.

- **Permanent marker (such as a Sharpie) or pencil:** to mark fusible web and template

- **Iron-off pen or pencil:** to mark fabric

- **Template interfacing**

- **Threads for appliqué**

- **Thread for machine quilting**

CUTTING

All measurements include ¼" seam allowances.

WHITE

- Cut 1 piece 40" × 40".

- Cut 1 strip 8½" × width of fabric; subcut 4 squares 8½" × 8½".

- Cut 4 strips 8½" × 41½".

DARK BLUE

- Cut 5 strips 2½" × width of fabric.

BINDING

- Cut 6 strips 2½" × width of fabric.

PREPARATION

Refer to How-To Instructions (pages 33–38) as needed.

1. Locate the *Blue Çini* Center Star pattern and pieces A1–2, B1–2, C, D1–2, E, Border Corner, and Border Crown on pullout page P4. Notice that these patterns are marked with the suggested blue for each piece: royal, dark, light, or pale blue. Refer to Creating a Project Outline Template (page 33) to make the template for your project. First, on the template interfacing use a permanent pen to mark a box that is 31″ × 31″. Mark through the center of this box with a horizontal line and vertical line as shown.

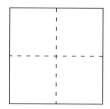

2. Only a quarter of the center star appliqué design pattern appears on the pullout page, so this pattern needs to be traced 4 times on the template interfacing to complete the center star. Line up the center star pattern in 1 quadrant of your marked square along the horizontal and vertical center lines. Trace the first quarter onto the template interfacing. Rotate the interfacing and realign the center lines. Repeat tracing the center design. Repeat 2 more times to create the full center star appliqué design. Be sure to also trace the labels *Traced Side for Fusible Web* and *Master Copy for Layout* (backward) on your template. For this quilt you make only this center star template to use for the layout. You will use the finished quilt photo (page 61) and the center panel layout diagram (page 64) as a guide for placement of the other appliqué elements.

3. Trace the remaining pattern design elements (apart from the center star template) onto the template interfacing, and label the templates with the location of each appliqué design and how many times it will be traced on fusible web as marked on the pattern.

4. Refer to the quilt photo (page 61) to view the dark blue band that creates the center star. Using the center star template, trace the edges of the star band (not the appliqué shapes on the star band) onto the paper side of the fusible web. If your fusible web is not large enough, join 2 pieces together. The center of the star band will be cut out, but you can use this center section of fusible web by tracing some appliqué elements that will use the same fabric into the very center of the star. Otherwise, this piece of fusible web will be discarded. (All the pieces will be cut out later.)

5. Refer to Tracing Designs onto Fusible Web (page 34). Using the templates (the center star template made in Step 2 and the templates made in Step 3), trace all the other needed appliqué templates onto the paper side of the fusible web using a permanent marker or pencil.

6. Cut the traced appliqué designs roughly, and divide them into piles to correspond with their chosen fabrics. If a group of appliqués are to be cut from the same fabric, you do not need to cut those apart. Follow the manufacturer's directions to fuse the fusible web onto the wrong side of the appropriate fabrics.

7. Cut each of the appliqué pieces on the traced lines.

CONSTRUCTION

Refer to How-To Instructions (pages 33–38) as needed.

Placing, Fusing, and Appliquéing

Because this is a fairly large project, you will position and fuse the appliqués in sections. Then you will machine appliqué one entire section before beginning the next section.

1. Use an iron-off pen to mark a square 37½″ × 37½″ in the center of the white 40″ × 40″ square. Mark through the center of this square with a horizontal line and vertical line as you did for the center star template. See Preparation, Step 1 (at left).

2. Align the center lines of the center star template with the center lines of the white 40″ × 40″ square.

3. Using the template, place and fuse the star band into place. Before adding any other appliqué pieces, machine appliqué the band.

4. Using the template again, place and fuse the appropriate appliqué elements within the star and on the star band. Machine appliqué these pieces.

$5.$ Refer to the quilt photo (page 61) and the center panel layout to guide the placement of the appliqué elements onto the center panel, staying inside the marked box of the white square. Fuse into place and machine appliqué.

Center panel layout

6. Mark the center of each white 8½″ × 41½″ piece. Use the diagram below as a placement guide for the border appliqué pieces on each of the 4 white strips. Fuse the appliqués into place. On the lower edge, align the raw edges of the appliqués with the raw edges of the border strips. Fuse and machine appliqué.

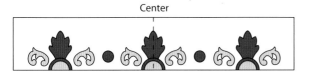

Center

7. The white 8½″ × 8½″ squares are the corner blocks of the final border. Mark the center of each square with drawn lines along the horizontal and vertical centers. Use these marks as a guide for placement of the appliqués. Fuse into place and machine appliqué.

Borders

1. Trim your center quilt panel to the 37½″ × 37½″ square that you originally marked.

2. Sew the dark blue 2½″ × width of fabric strips together end to end. Then cut 4 border strips 2½″ × 45″.

3. Refer to Mitering the Borders (page 39) and sew the dark blue 2½″ × 45″ strips onto the center panel with mitered corners.

4. Sew appliquéd border strips to opposite sides of the quilt center, and press the seams toward the border pieces.

5. Sew an appliquéd 8½″ square to each end of the remaining appliquéd border strips. Press the seams toward the border strip.

6. Pin the 2 border pieces to the top and bottom of the quilt, lining up the seams carefully. Sew and press.

Finishing

1. Layer the quilt top, the batting, and the backing. Quilt as desired.

2. Use the binding 2½″ strips to finish the quilt.

TOPKAPI

FINISHED SIZE:
40″ × 48½″
(102cm × 122cm)

Fabrics featured in this quilt are from the Shadow Play collection by Maywood Studios. The white background fabric is from the Pearl Essence collection from Galaxy Fabrics.

The Topkapı Palace, located in Istanbul, was the primary home of the sultans from 1465 until 1856. The palace complex consists of four main courtyards, the harem, and many small buildings. It was not only the main residence of the sultan and his court, but was also initially the seat of government in which the imperial court met and conducted business. The palace was designed to provide the sultan with privacy and discretion. Today, as a museum, it is an example of the lifestyle of the sultan and his court. Rooms are heavily decorated with gold accents, İznik tiles, upholsteries, and luxury items. Large panels of İznik tiles, still in impeccable condition, are located throughout the palace. Numerous pavilions, chambers, kiosks, dormitories, and gardens, along with the harem, look out over the Bosphorus and Istanbul. This quilt is inspired by several of the panels located within the palace.

MATERIALS

Yardage is based on 42"-wide fabric.

- **White:** 1 yard (95cm) for background

- **Pale green:** ¼ yard (25cm) for inside border

- **Dark blue:** 1⅞ yards (171cm) for outside border and binding

- **Backing:** 3 yards (274cm)

- **Batting:** 46" × 57" (110cm × 135cm)

- **Fusible web:** 2 yards (183cm) × 18" wide (46cm)

- **Permanent marker (such as a Sharpie) or pencil:** to mark fusible web and template

- **Iron-off pen or pencil:** to mark fabric

- **Template interfacing**

- **Threads for appliqué**

- **Thread for machine quilting**

FOR APPLIQUÉS:

(You will only need ¼ yard or less of some of the fabrics below. Scraps in your stash will often work well for these appliqués.)

- **Aqua:** ¼ yard (25cm) for flowers

- **Brown:** ⅓ yard (30cm) for stems

- **Reds:** ¼ yard (25cm) total of 2 different reds for flowers

- **Blues:** ¼ yard (25cm) total of 5 different blues for flowers

- **Greens:** ½ yard (45cm) total of 7 different greens for leaves

- **Very dark blue:** 12" × 10" (30cm × 25cm) for vase

- **Pale green:** 5" × 5" (13cm) for vase

- **Cream:** ⅛ yard for flowers

- **Gold:** ⅛ yard for flowers

CUTTING

All measurements include ¼" seam allowances.

WHITE
- Cut 1 piece 30" × 38½".

PALE GREEN
- Cut 4 strips 1½" × width of fabric.

DARK BLUE
- Cut 4 strips 6½" × 65", *parallel to selvage edge.*

- Cut 3 strips 2½" × length of fabric, *parallel to selvage edge.*

PREPARATION

Refer to How-To Instructions (pages 33–38) as needed.

1. Locate the *Topkapı* pattern on pullout page P1. Refer to Creating a Project Outline Template (page 33). On the template interfacing, mark a box 26″ × 34½″. Align the edges of the box marked with the appliqué design, and trace the entire pattern into place on the template interfacing. Be sure to trace the labels *Traced Side for Fusible Web* and *Master Copy for Layout* (backward) on your template.

2. Refer to Tracing Designs onto Fusible Web (page 34). Using the Traced Side of the template, trace the required number of the appliqué designs onto the paper side of the fusible web using a permanent marker or pencil. (You will need 24 complete units of the 3-piece aqua, cream, and gold flowers.)

3. Cut the traced appliqué designs roughly, and divide them into piles to correspond with their chosen fabrics. If a group of appliqués will be cut from the same fabric, you do not need to cut those apart. Follow the manufacturer's directions to fuse the fusible web onto the wrong side of the appropriate fabrics.

4. Cut each of the appliqué pieces on the traced lines.

CONSTRUCTION

Refer to How-To Instructions (pages 33–38) as needed.

Placing and Fusing the Appliqué Pieces

1. In the center of the white 30″ × 38½″ piece, mark a box 26″ × 34½″, using an iron-off pen or pencil.

2. Assemble and fuse the flowers, which have several parts. Refer to Fusing Multipiece Flowers (page 36). You may want to hand or machine appliqué the smaller parts to the larger flower bases before they are fused to the large background.

3. Matching the lines of the template box with the drawn lines on the white background, use the Master Copy side of your template to place the appliqué pieces onto the white background fabric. Fuse your appliqué pieces into place.

Appliqué

Refer to Machine Appliqué (page 38) as needed.

Use your preferred method to appliqué around each of the pieces.

Borders

1. Trim the center panel on the drawn lines of the box. Use the Master Copy template to redraw the lines if needed.

2. Mark the center points of the 4 pale green 1½″ × width of fabric strips and the 4 dark blue 6½″ × 65″ strips.

3. Sew a pale green strip to a dark blue strip, matching the centers. Press the seam toward the dark blue. Repeat to make 4 border units.

4. Refer to Mitering the Borders (page 39) and sew the border units onto the center panel with mitered corners.

Finishing

1. Layer the quilt top, the batting, and the backing. Quilt as desired.

2. Use the dark blue 2½″ strips to bind the quilt.

THE PEACOCK

FINISHED SIZE:
35″ × 47″
(89cm × 119cm)

The Tree of Life symbol is found in many cultures throughout history. It appears in Turkic mythology because the Turks believed human beings descended from the trees. The peacock was an exotic bird and has often been linked to royalty. This quilt is inspired by several ceramic plates created by the İznik artists, one of which can be found in the British Museum in London. The border design is inspired by both the palmetto tree branches and the lotus flower—a symbol of transition from sunrise to sunset, as the flower opens at sunrise and closes at sunset.

MATERIALS

Yardage is based on 42"-wide fabric.

- **Dark blue:** 2¼ yards (160cm) for background and binding

- **White:** ⅞ yard (80cm) for border and flowers

- **Backing:** 1½ yards (135cm)

- **Batting:** 41" × 53" (110cm × 135cm)

- **Fusible web:** 2½ yards (229cm) × 18" wide (46cm)

- **Permanent marker (such as a Sharpie) or pencil:** to mark fusible web and template

- **Iron-off pen or pencil:** to mark fabric

- **Template interfacing**

- **Threads for appliqué**

- **Thread for machine quilting**

FOR APPLIQUÉS:

- **Brown:** ⅓ yard (30cm) for tree stems

- **Gold:** ⅛ yard (12cm) for flower centers and border appliqués

- **Greens:** ¼ yard (25cm) total of different greens for leaves

- **Light blue:** ⅓ yard (30cm) for flowers in border and tree

- **Aquas:**
  ⅛ yard (12cm) total of light and dark for border appliqués

  ¼ yard (25cm) total of light and dark for peacock feathers*

- **Cream:** small scraps for peacock's legs

- **Black:** small scrap for peacock's eye

* Refer to Fabrics (page 30) to see how I did my peacock body feathers, fussy cutting them from one fabric.

CUTTING

All measurements include ¼" seam allowances.

DARK BLUE

- Cut 1 piece 35" × 39".

- Cut 2 pieces 8½" × 38".

- Cut 5 strips 2½" × width of fabric.

WHITE

- Cut 2 pieces 6½" × 38".

FUSIBLE WEB

- Cut 2 strips 6½" × 38".

PREPARATION

Refer to How-To Instructions (pages 33–38) as needed.

Center Panel

1. Locate *The Peacock* Center Panel pattern on pullout page P2. Refer to Creating a Project Outline Template (page 33) to make the templates for your project. On the template interfacing, mark a box 35" × 31". (This is the correct orientation to position the pattern.) Mark the center of this box with a horizontal line and vertical line. Align the center of the panel pattern with the center on the template. Trace the panel pattern onto the template interfacing. Be sure to trace the labels *Traced Side for Fusible Web* and *Master Copy for Layout* (backward) on your template.

2. Using the Traced Side of the panel template and a permanent pen, trace all the appliqué pieces onto the paper side of the fusible web. (You will need 41 complete flower blossoms of white, aqua, and gold layers for the panel.) Before you trace all the feathers separately, refer to Fabrics (page 30) to see how I did my peacock body feathers, fussy cutting them from 1 fabric instead of individual pieces from several different fabrics.

3. Cut the traced appliqué designs roughly, and divide them into piles to correspond with their chosen fabrics. If a group of appliqués will be cut from the same fabric, you do not need to cut those apart. Follow the manufacturer's directions to fuse the fusible web onto the wrong side of the appropriate fabrics.

4. Cut each of the appliqué pieces on the traced lines. Keep these pieces together for the center panel.

Border

1. Locate *The Peacock* Border pattern and border pieces A, B, and C on pullout page P2. Refer to Creating a Project Outline Template (page 33) to make the templates for your project. Using a permanent pen, trace the border section and A, B, and C pieces on template interfacing. Label the template with the number of pieces required as marked on the pattern page. You do not have to label this template as Traced Side or Master Copy side, because the patterns are symmetrical and do not create mirror images when turned from one side to another. You can trace from either side of this template.

2. Using the A, B, and C templates and a permanent pen, trace the required number of A, B, and C pieces onto the paper side of the fusible web.

3. Cut the traced appliqué designs roughly, and divide them into piles to correspond with their chosen fabrics. If a group of appliqués will be cut from the same fabric, you do not need to cut those apart. Follow the manufacturer's directions to fuse the fusible web onto the wrong side of the appropriate fabrics.

4. To make the continuous border template, align the center of the border template with the center of the fusible 6½" × 38" strip, with the top and bottom edges even. Trace the border template without drawing vertical lines at either end. Realign the template to the left to continue the pattern, and trace 2 more times, drawing a vertical line at the left end of the template. Realign the template to the right of the original tracing, and trace 2 more times, drawing a vertical line on the right end. Do not trim the ends of the fusible strip beyond the tracing. Repeat on the other fusible web 6½" × 38" strip.

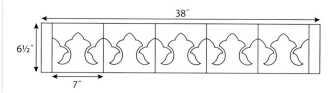

5. Follow the manufacturer's directions to fuse the fusible web border strips to the wrong side of the white 6½" × 38" strips.

6. Carefully cut the drawn center line the length of both fused strips. Do not trim the ends of the border strips. Keep only the lower sections of the border strips.

CONSTRUCTION

Refer to How-To Instructions (pages 33–38) as needed.

Placing, Fusing, and Appliquéing the Center Panel

1. Use an iron-off pen to mark the dark blue 39″ × 35″ piece with a box 35″ × 31″ in the center of the fabric. Mark the center of the box with reference lines on the horizontal and vertical centers.

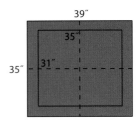

2. Remove the backing paper from the fused appliqués. Refer to Fusing Multipiece Flowers (page 36). You may want to hand or machine appliqué the smaller parts to the larger flower bases before fusing them to the large background.

3. Using the Master Copy side of the center panel template, match the center reference lines on the Master Copy side of the template with the center reference lines on the dark blue background. Then position the appliqué pieces following the template. When fusing the center feathers into place, place the outermost parts first, followed by the inner pieces, with the round part of the feather positioned on top. Fuse your appliqué pieces into place.

4. Use your preferred method to appliqué around each of the pieces on the panel.

Placing, Fusing, and Appliquéing the Borders

1. Remove the backing from the white appliqué border strips. Fuse a white border strip on a dark blue 8½″ × 38″ strip, aligning the bottom edges. Repeat with the other border pieces.

2. Remove the backing paper from the border appliqué pieces. Refer to the project photo (page 70) for the layout to arrange the pieces on the white appliqué strips, and fuse into place.

3. Use your preferred method to appliqué around each of the appliqué pieces on the borders.

4. Trim the length of the borders to 35″, measuring 17½″ from the center of each strip.

Borders

1. Trim the center panel on the marked lines 35″ × 31″.

2. Position the top and bottom border strips with the white touching the dark blue center panel. Sew the border strips to the center.

Finishing

1. Layer the quilt top, the batting, and the backing. Quilt as desired.

2. Use the dark blue 2½″ strips to bind the quilt.

ISTANBUL

Hand appliquéd by Angela Perry, machine quilted by Tamsin Harvey. Fabrics featured in this quilt are from the Shadow Play collection by Maywood Studio. The white background is from the Pearl Essence collection from Galaxy Fabrics.

FINISHED SIZE:
62″ × 62″
(157cm × 157cm)

This quilt was inspired by the numerous İznik tile designs that include floral sprays of tulips, carnations, roses, peonies, and violets. The tulip created a craze within the Ottoman court society between 1718 and 1730. During the reign of Sultan Ahmed III, improving trade relations and developing commercial revenues was of major interest. There was a return to the gardens, and tulips were a favorite of the Ottoman court. Tulips appear often in Ottoman art from this period, not only in the decoration of İznik tiles, but also in carpets and paintings.

MATERIALS

Yardage is based on 42"-wide fabric.

- **Red:** 2½ yards (183cm) for inside and outside borders

- **White:** 1⅝ yards (149cm) for center background and inside border

- **Binding:** ⅝ yard (55cm)

- **Backing:** 3¾ yards (345cm)

- **Batting:** 68" × 68"

- **Fusible web:** 3 yards (274cm) at least 18" wide (46cm)

- **Permanent marker (such as a Sharpie) or pencil:** to mark fusible web and template

- **Iron-off pen or pencil:** to mark fabric

- **Template interfacing**

- **Threads for appliqué**

- **Thread for machine quilting**

FOR APPLIQUÉS:

- **Greens:** ½ yard (45cm) total of 3 different greens for leaves

- **Reds:** ½ yard (45cm) total of 2 different reds for flowers

- **Dark blue:** ¼ yard (25cm) for flowers

- **Light blue:** ¼ yard (25cm) for flowers

- **Brown:** ¼ yard (25cm) for stems

- **Cream:** small scrap for flower centers

CUTTING

All measurements include ¼" seam allowances.

RED

- Cut 5 strips 2" × width of fabric.

- Cut 4 strips 8½" × 68" length of fabric, *parallel to selvage edge.*

WHITE

- Cut 1 square 41" × 41".

- Cut 6 strips 1½" × width of fabric.

BINDING

- Cut 7 strips 2½" × width of fabric.

PREPARATION

Refer to How-To Instructions (pages 33–38) as needed.

1. Locate the *Istanbul* pattern on pullout page P4. Refer to Creating a Project Outline Template (page 33). On the template interfacing, trace the appliqué pattern with the guide side marks, using a permanent marker. Be sure to trace the labels *Traced Side for Fusible Web* and *Master Copy for Layout* (backward) on your template.

2. The pattern represents ⅛ of the design, so it will be used 8 times to complete the project. Using the Traced Side of your template, trace the required number of the appliqué designs onto the paper side of the fusible web, using a permanent marker or pencil. (You will need 24 complete small blossom flowers of the light blue, dark blue, and white fabric.)

3. Cut around each of the traced appliqué designs roughly, and divide them into piles to correspond with their chosen fabrics. If a group of appliqués will be cut from the same fabric, you do not need to cut those apart. Follow the manufacturer's directions to fuse the fusible web onto the wrong side of the fabric.

4. Cut around each of the appliqué pieces on the traced lines.

CONSTRUCTION

Refer to How-To Instructions (pages 33–38) as needed.

Placing, Fusing, and Appliquéing

1. The white 41″ × 41″ square is to be divided into 8 segments. Use an iron-off pen or pencil to mark the background square with drawn lines as shown.

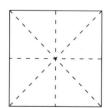

2. Remove the backing paper from the fused appliqués. Using the Master Copy side of the template, place the appliqué pieces onto 1 segment of the background. Refer to Fusing Multipiece Flowers (page 36) for the blossom flowers. You may want to hand or machine appliqué the smaller parts to the larger flower bases before fusing them to the large background.

3. As this is a large quilt with many different appliqués, I advise you to work on 1 segment at a time. Fuse this segment and appliqué, then move onto the next segment and repeat. Use your preferred method to appliqué around each of the appliqué pieces. Refer to Machine Appliqué (page 38) as needed.

Borders

1. Sew the 5 red 2″ × width of fabric strips together end to end. Cut 4 strips 2″ × 50″.

2. Sew the 6 white 1½″ × width of fabric strips together end to end. Then cut 4 strips 1½″ × 52″.

3. Mark the center points of the 4 red 2″ × 50″ strips, the 4 white 1½″ × 52″ strips, and the 4 red 8½″ × 68″ strips.

4. Matching the center points, sew a red 2″ strip to a white 1½″ strip. Make 4 red/white units. Press the seams toward the red.

5. Matching the center points, sew a red/white unit to a red 8½″ strip with the white strip against the red 8½″ strip. Make 4 red/white/red units. Press the seams toward the red.

6. Refer to Mitering the Borders (page 39) and sew the borders onto the center panel with mitered corners.

Finishing

1. Layer the quilt top, the batting, and the backing. Quilt as desired.

2. Use the binding 2½″ strips to finish the quilt.

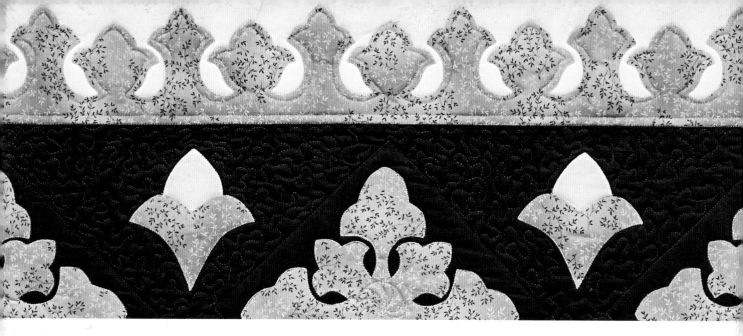

SUPPLIES AND RESOURCES

Many of the products suggested in this book are readily available. As a retail patchwork shop owner, I encourage you to purchase supplies from your local quilt shop. If they don't have a particular item in stock, they will often be willing to place a special order for it. Please support your local quilt shop because without your support, that shop would not be there.

A Bernina 750QE was used to machine appliqué and machine quilt the projects in this book.

For further details about Bernina sewing machines, please visit:

Bernina • bernina.com

For further education about threads, sewing machine tension, and machine needles, please visit:

Superior Threads • superiorthreads.com

TILE PHOTO LOCATIONS IN ISTANBUL, TURKEY

Eyüp Sultan Mosque

Hagia Sophia Museum • ayasofyamuzesi.gov.tr/en

Rüstem Pasha Mosque

Sultanahmet Mosque (Blue Mosque) • bluemosque.co

Topkapı Palace Museum • topkapisarayi.gov.tr/en

BIBLIOGRAPHY

Akar, Azade. *Authentic Turkish Designs*. Dover Publications, 1992.

Denny, Walter B. *Iznik: The Artistry of Ottoman Ceramics*. Thames & Hudson, 2005.

Carswell, John. *Iznik Pottery (Eastern Art)*. Interlink Books, 2006.

Capucho, Maria d'Orey. *Iznik Pottery and Tiles: In the Calouste Gulbenkian Collection*. Scala Publishers Ltd., 2010.

Weissenbacher, Edda Renker. *A Self-Guide to Iznik Tiles in Istanbul*. Published by author, 2004.

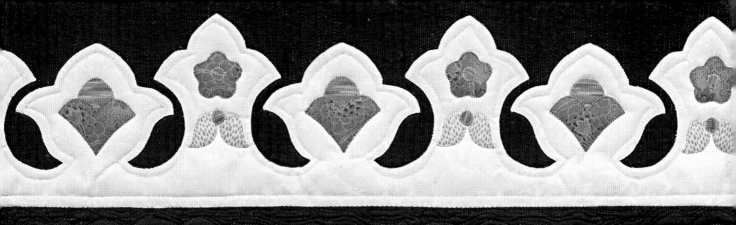

ABOUT THE AUTHOR

Tamsin Harvey grew up around sewing and fabric as a result of a family-owned business. Sewing has been part of her life since an early age.

It was not until later, however, that her quilting journey began by chance when she was visiting a close relative who was a hand quilter with a large collection of quilts. Amazed by these quilts, Tamsin started to quilt by machine and has been addicted ever since.

In 2007, Tamsin and her mother, Sue, purchased Berrima Patchwork, a quilting and fabric store in the Southern Highlands of New South Wales, Australia. Because of demand in the store, she started to design her own patterns and teach workshops.

She is the designer and owner of the pattern company Berrima Design. Her designs have appeared in several Australian patchwork magazines, including *Quilter's Companion*, *Australian Homespun*, and *Down Under Quilts*.

Tamsin's other passion (when time permits) is traveling to exotic and historic countries, which inspire her quilting designs. Tamsin lives in the Southern Highlands, an hour and a half southwest of Sydney, with her two Maine Coon feline "quilting consultants," Phoenix and Indiana.

Great Titles *from* C&T PUBLISHING

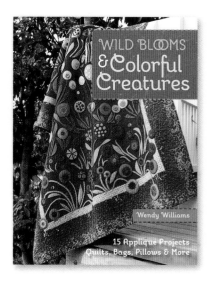

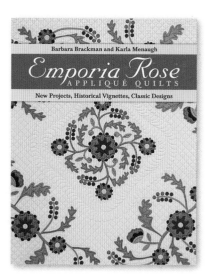

Available at your local retailer or **ctpub.com** *or* **800-284-1114**

For a list of other fine books from C&T Publishing, visit our website
to view our catalog online.

C&T PUBLISHING, INC.

P.O. Box 1456
Lafayette, CA 94549
800-284-1114

Email: ctinfo@ctpub.com
Website: ctpub.com

Tips and Techniques can be found at ctpub.com/quilting-sewing-tips.

For quilting supplies:

COTTON PATCH

1025 Brown Ave.
Lafayette, CA 94549
Store: 925-284-1177
Mail order: 925-283-7883

Email: CottonPa@aol.com
Website: quiltusa.com

Note: Fabrics shown may not be currently available, as fabric
manufacturers keep most fabrics in print for only a short time.